SALT AND LIGHT
POCKET GUIDES

COMING TO GRIPS WITH
GOD'S
DISCIPLINE
OF THE
BELIEVER

COMING TO GRIPS WITH GOD'S DISCIPLINE OF THE BELIEVER

ERWIN W. LUTZER

MOODY PRESS
CHICAGO

Coming to Grips with

God's Discipline
of the Believer

One of the most important responsibilities a father has is to
discipline his children. A father who
does not take this responsibility seri-
ously is negligent and does not love
his children as he ought.

Though God is the Father of all
men, He has a special filial relationship to those who have been born into
His family through faith in Christ Jesus. Paul the apostle encourages us to
develop intimacy with our Heavenly
Father: "For you have not received a
spirit of slavery leading to fear again,
but you have received a spirit of adop-
tion as sons by which we cry out, 'Abba!
Father!'" (Romans 8:15).

That God disciplines His children is not in doubt, but how He does
is not always clear to us. We are espe-
cially confused when we try to find a

link between a particular transgression and God's disciplinary response.

When a couple, whom I shall call Sally and John, had a deformed baby born to them, they asked a question that we all would likely have asked in their situation: "What did we do to deserve this?"

Eventually, they accepted their bitter disappointment as a judgment from God because they had had premarital sex. The chickens were coming home to roost, they thought.

Yet, when the baby grew up to be a special blessing despite his handicap, they wondered whether they were right in their original assumption about the discipline of God.

William Carey, the famous missionary, spent forty years in India starting churches and doing translation work. Thousands of painstaking hours were invested learning the vocabulary and grammar of strange languages and compiling them into a massive dictionary. But this, along with other of his priceless manuscripts, was destroyed in a warehouse fire in 1812. A lesser man may have never recovered, but Carey accepted this as a judgment from God (perhaps because of his failures as a father) and began the task all over again with even greater zeal.

One Christian woman I know chose to ignore the counsel of the elders in her church and decided to divorce her husband on the grounds of incompatibility. A month later she took sick and nearly died. She interpreted the illness as a direct judgment from God for her rebellion.

We've all entertained the suspicion that one of these days God will get even for our misdeeds. It is natural to interpret our tragedies in light of our past sins and blame ourselves for what has happened. We remind ourselves that the hand of the Lord is against those who do evil.

Though Christians are opposed to the pantheistic doctrine of Karma, we do believe in a general law of cause and effect. Paul wrote, "Do not be deceived, God is not mocked; for whatever a man sows, this he will also reap" (Galatians 6:7). This, we think, gives us the right to interpret the tragedies of life as a judgment for specific sins and failures.

Yet, when we stop to think of how and when God disciplines us, we immediately face some rather puzzling questions.

First, is He not inconsistent? In all three instances given above, we can think of other people who were guilty of the same sins and failures, yet they did not experience God's discipline (or at least they did not have the same tragedies come to them).

Some Christians have premarital sex, others fail in raising their children, and still others divorce for no reason, yet these believers live without apparent hardship.

As parents we have been taught to treat all of our children alike; the experts tell us that there must be consistent discipline. But our Heavenly Father seems to disregard this fundamental rule. Document the lives of both His faithful and unfaithful servants and virtually no pattern of discipline is readily discernible.

A second question: How can one be sure of the connection between a particular sin and the discipline? In each of the instances mentioned above, the people involved had other sins or weaknesses in their lives that could have accounted for the discipline. The relationship between sin and its consequences is not always easy to detect.

In this age of grace most of us give little thought to the discipline of the Lord until tragedy strikes. Then we begin to ask whether there is a connection between our sin and the heartaches of life.

To probe this topic we must study God's discipline from a broad perspective and then narrow our focus to try to answer the puzzling questions we have raised.

The people to whom the book of Hebrews was written were experiencing persecution; indeed, they were on the verge of having to die for their faith. They had joyfully endured the seizure of their property and identified themselves with prisoners of the Lord. This meant increased persecution. But it was becoming wearisome; some wanted to give up their Christian witness.

God speaks to them:

> You have not yet resisted to the point of shedding blood in your striving against sin; and you have forgotten the exhortation which is addressed to you as sons, "My son do not regard lightly the discipline of the Lord, nor faint when you are reproved by Him; for those whom the Lord loves He disciplines, and He scourges every son whom He receives." It is for discipline that you endure; God deals with you as with sons; for what son is there whom his father does not discipline? But if you are without discipline of which all have become partakers, then you are illegitimate children and not sons. (Hebrews 12:4-8)

The text could not be clearer: the basis of discipline is sonship. Every one of God's sons is disciplined; indeed, scourging is proof of sonship. We usually think that God should prove His love by delivering us from the hardships of life. Actually, the opposite is the case: these trials prove His love.

We must make a distinction between the way God treats His children as opposed to His relationship to unbelievers. Strictly speaking, God's children never come under His wrath, for they have been shielded from His judicial anger through the redemption of Christ. "There is therefore now no condemnation for those who are in Christ Jesus" (Romans 8:1).

All sin must be paid for. Those who reject the sacrifice of Christ end up bearing the weight of their own sin. And because there is no human suffering that can pay the debt, the condemnation goes on forever.

But those who accept the sacrifice of Christ for themselves are shielded from His wrath. The doctrine of grace teaches that we do not have to get what we deserve.

Thus, although God punishes His enemies, He chastises His children. We must think of this discipline as correction, not condemnation. The Greek word used in the text of Hebrews is *paideia* (from *pais*, child) and refers to instruction. Charles Bridges wrote, "The same hand—but not the same character—gives the stroke to the godly and ungodly. The scourge of the Judge is widely different from the rod of the Father" (*Commentary on Proverbs*, p. 31).

If God didn't discipline His children He would be a negligent father. He would be displaying cruel disinterest if He were indifferent to whether his children obeyed or not.

In ancient cultures it was unthinkable that a father would not discipline his children. Indeed, the Roman father had total authority over his son, even to the point of being able to execute him if he desired. Such harsh, uncaring discipline is in contrast to that of the heavenly Father, who disciplines us from the standpoint of love and wisdom. His discipline may appear harsh, but it is not based on the misjudgments an earthly father might make.

Our heavenly Father is so consistent in His discipline that not even his beloved Son escaped the scourging that all sons need as they develop toward maturity. "Although He was a Son, He learned obedience from the things which He suffered. And having been made perfect, He became to all those who obey Him the source of eternal salvation" (Hebrews 5:8-9). What this means will be clarified later.

Clearly, there are no exceptions. Every son whom the Father receives is scourged. Far from being inconsistent, our heavenly Father takes great pains not to overlook any of His children.

Two implications follow. First, discipline is a sign of sonship. If we are without discipline, we are illegitimate. We are not born of God the Father but only claim to be.

In practical terms this means that if someone says that he or she is a Christian and lives in sin without any form of discipline, such a person is probably deceived. Since God holds earthly fathers accountable for punishing and admonishing rebellious children, we cannot expect that He would do anything less.

Discipline is not an optional course in God's curriculum; it is required. Just as an oak tree cannot grow without wind, so we cannot become mature without the benefit of scourging.

Second, discipline is a sign of love. We usually think just the opposite, namely, that discipline is a sign of God's anger and displeasure. "Why does God turn against me when I need Him the most?" we ask, as if God's primary motivation is a morbid desire to make life difficult for us and "even the score" at every turn. But God's discipline toward His children is not motivated by revenge, but love.

There is no doubt that God desires to glorify Himself through the lives of His children. But He does not arbitrarily give us difficult circumstances simply to please Himself. We must not lose sight of the fact that discipline is actually for our good.

We've all told our children, "This spanking hurts me more than it does you!" I'm not sure that this is true (at least my children didn't believe me), but the sentiment expressed is that no responsible parent disciplines his children arbitrarily. It is done with the best interest of the child in mind.

One woman, who when told that her tragedies were the result of God's love for her, responded by saying, "I wish He wouldn't love me so much!" But God loves all of us equally in Christ. Some are called upon to suffer more than others, but they should not attribute such suffering to God's loving them too much. Life is filled with injustices and tragedies that appear to come indiscriminately to the godly as well as the ungodly.

It is better to try to learn the lessons God has in mind for us than to blame our lot in life to a higher degree of love. What is important is to realize that that which comes to believers first passes through God's loving hands.

The basis of discipline is sonship. Our sufferings are appointed for our good and God's glory.

Unfortunately, we usually think of discipline only as God's immediate response to specific sins. But the Bible teaches that our heavenly Father has a more comprehensive curriculum.

EDUCATIVE DISCIPLINE

Frequently, God disciplines us to deepen our relationship with Him. This kind of discipline has no direct relationship to specific sins.

One example is Job, who experienced tragedy, not because he was a great sinner, but because he was righteous. The Lord taunted Satan, "Have you considered my servant Job? For there is no one like him on the earth, a blameless and upright man, fearing God and turning away from evil" (Job 1:8).

Job was put on trial before Satan, angels, and God to see what he would do when faith in God no longer seemed to be beneficial. Satan said that Job was righteous only because of the blessings that were coming to him because of his piety. God had given him a fine family, wealth, and health. But if these were removed, said the devil, Job would curse God to His face.

The rest of the book of Job shows that although Job was considered righteous, he was not perfect. The trial brought needed refinements, along with a new appreciation for God's sovereignty. He was disciplined to be educated and refined.

Job's three friends made the mistake of thinking that there was always a direct relationship between a man's circumstances and his piety. If Job were righteous, they argued, the tragedies he experienced would not have happened. But they were wrong. Many trials are designed to educate us; they are not the result of specific sins. In other words, we cannot tell the righteous from the wicked by checking the size of their bank accounts or their medical records.

An even clearer example was Christ Himself, who was disciplined not because of sin but because He needed to prove His obedience to the will of the Father. Indeed, Christ was not only sinless, but most theologians believe He was incapable of sin. We might think that since He was the special Son of God it would be beyond His dignity to suffer. Yet we read that He learned obedience by the things that He suffered: "And having been made perfect, He became to all those who obey Him the source of eternal salvation" (Hebrews 5:9).

The discipline was not that His Person might be made perfect but that He might become perfected in His work, the assignment of the cross.

Thus He "learned obedience by the things which He suffered." The result was that He became the author of eternal salvation to all who believe.

Usually we think of discipline only as the response of a parent to disobedience. We must broaden our understanding to include the "disciplines" that are needed for all of us to develop in spiritual maturity. James wrote, "And let endurance have its perfect result, that you may be perfect and complete, lacking in nothing" (James 1:4).

When tragedy strikes we cannot always assume that we can trace it to specific sins or failures. That was precisely the error of Job's three friends, who thought that there was a direct correlation between the greatness of one's sin and the greatness of one's personal calamity. But the book of Job ends by proving that God puts some of His most obedient children through the severest trials.

PREVENTATIVE DISCIPLINE

This kind of hardship is brought into our lives to keep us from impending sin. Paul was given a thorn in the flesh, a messenger of Satan. The reason for this trial was that he had been given many special revelations from God and therefore faced the temptation of exalting himself.

He writes: "And because of the surpassing greatness of revelations, for this reason, to keep me from exalting myself, there was given me a thorn in the flesh, a messenger of Satan to buffet me—to keep me from exalting myself!" (2 Corinthians 12:7).

If we object to this kind of discipline on the grounds that we are being spanked for something we haven't done yet, we overlook the fact that our heavenly Father knows all things and therefore does not have to wait to see how we will react in a specific situation. An earthly father might not have the right to give us preventative discipline, but our heavenly Father sees us from an omniscient perspective.

This kind of discipline fulfills the prayer "Lead us not into temptation, but deliver us from evil." We should ask God to bring roadblocks into our lives that will keep us from sin. The pain of a trial is much better than the wreckage of a ruined life or ministry.

Billy Graham was asked how he remained humble in the face of so much favorable publicity. He replied by enumerating all of the physical ailments he had experienced, from broken ribs to the pain of phlebitis. Like Paul, he was given a thorn in the flesh, a preventative discipline, to keep him from sin.

We will probably never know how many sins we have been kept

from because of the preventative discipline of God. Even a lack of funds, the pressure of a busy schedule, and ill health—these and other trials may be used of God to keep us from temptations that would be too hard for us to resist. Our heavenly Father knows what is best for us.

RETRIBUTIVE DISCIPLINE

Sometimes discipline does come as a result of specific sins. Though David confessed his sin of murder and adultery, the Lord said, "Now therefore, the sword shall never depart from your house, because you have despised Me and have taken the wife of Uriah the Hittite to be your wife" (2 Samuel 12:10). Then followed additional judgments: (1) his wives would be publicly humiliated and (2) the child that Bathsheba would bear would die.

All of this, even though David had confessed his sin and was forgiven by God. There are consequences that precede confession and there are others that follow. Here we have a direct cause-effect relationship between sin and punishment.

The Israelites were also forgiven by God, but they were condemned to wander in the desert because of their unbelief at Kadesh-barnea. "Say to them, 'As I live,' says the Lord, 'just as you have spoken in My hearing, so I will surely do to you; your corpses shall fall in this wilderness, even all your numbered men, according to your complete number from twenty years old and upward, who have grumbled against Me'" (Numbers 14:28-29).

Jonah ended up in the belly of a fish because he rebelled against God's instructions. He was given a plant to shade him from the blistering sun; then it was taken away to test his priorities. All of this, because of his disobedience.

Identifying the relationship between our sin and the discipline that follows is often difficult, though in some instances it is quite clear. Later I shall give some suggestions as to how we can try to discern the intention of the Almighty.

THE PURPOSE OF DISCIPLINE

Think back to when you were a child and you received discipline. What was its purpose?

The author of the book of Hebrews continues his discourse by saying, "Furthermore, we had earthly fathers to discipline us, and we respected them; shall we not much rather be subject to the Father of spirits and live? For they disciplined us for a short time as seemed best to them, but He disciplines us for our good, that we may share His holiness" (Hebrews 12:9-10).

Our earthly fathers disciplined us according to their best judgment (there are exceptions, of course), and we responded with respect and obedience. But God disciplines us with unerring discernment and knowledge. He not only has greater wisdom but also a greater purpose.

The specific purpose of the discipline is to motivate us to pursue a deeper relationship with God. There is no doubt that God's hand is often painful, but hurting produces holiness. Indeed, we "share His holiness."

What are the requirements for holiness?

The first is submission. We are to be "subject to the Father of spirits." The phrase "Father of spirits" is an unusual expression found only here in Scripture. Perhaps it means simply, "Our spiritual Father." But when we submit to Him, we "live." The implication is that if we don't submit we might die (as we shall see, there is a sin unto death), or perhaps the author means that we enter into a new quality of life here on earth. Either way we benefit.

Every time we were disciplined as children we could either rebel or yield to our father's hand. The discipline either softened us or made us more rebellious. Thus God frequently increases the doses, intending to bring us to a state of complete yieldedness.

Second, discipline requires our loyalty. It is said that when there is a storm at sea sailors either turn to God or to drink. Every person, at some time, comes to the crunch and must choose where he will turn.

I have just spoken to a man who works in a firm where there is not only much bickering but where each of the employees undercuts the others in an attempt to jockey for power and position. This Christian man is trying to learn how to fulfill the admonition of Scripture "Never take your own revenge, beloved, but leave room for the wrath of God, for it is written, 'Vengeance is Mine, I will repay,' says the Lord" (Romans 12:19). The test of his loyalty to God is this: Can he entrust his complaints to God or must he take matters into his own hand? Virtually every trial of life forces us to choose between loyalty to ourselves or loyalty to God.

When Abraham was asked to offer Isaac as a sacrifice, he successfully faced this supreme test by God. Generations to come would stand in awe of what a man was willing to do for God. No question as to where his loyalty stood.

A third requirement is fear. Yes, that's right, fear. Obedience has its reward, but so does disobedience. The child who has been to God's wood-shed and felt the pain of his disobedience is in no mood for a repeat performance. "Before I was afflicted I went astray, but now I keep Thy Word" (Psalm 119:67).

When there has been an offense, discipline always includes restoration. A good father will not only spank his children but will also comfort them once they have yielded to his authority. Though it hurts for a time, later this discipline yields the "peaceable fruit of righteousness" (Hebrews 12:11, KJV*).

We've all been able to identify a child because he resembled his father. In fact, if there were no likeness we might be tempted to suppose that the child was illegitimate, conceived by another man. There are Christians whose family pedigree is suspect because they are so unlike our heavenly Father.

When we pray, "Oh, Father, make me godly," we mean, "make me God-like." Christ taught us the reason we should love our enemies: it is so that "your reward will be great, and you will be sons of the Most High; for He Himself is kind to ungrateful and evil men. Be merciful, just as your Father is merciful." (Luke 6:35*b*-36). The au-

* King James Version

22

thor of Hebrews says that we are to "share His holiness" (Hebrews 12:10).

Discipline should lead us to *a greater degree of family resemblance.* When we were disciplined by our parents the intention (it is hoped) was that we would have the same character traits of honesty and obedience that they had.

We should live up to the family name.

THE METHODS OF DISCIPLINE

God deals with His children in a variety of ways, depending on what is needed to bring about repentance and restoration.

All sin has built-in consequences of some kind. Since God has set up the moral system of the universe, it is unthinkable that any sin could be intrinsically free from detrimental effects. To these, God adds His own incentives to bring us to our senses and respond to the prompting of the Holy Spirit.

THE CONTINUING CONSEQUENCE OF SIN

The familiar illustration of nails that leave holes even after being pulled out of a barn door is to the point of our discussion of discipline for sin. The thief, if discovered, must go to prison; the child killed by an alcoholic driver can never be resurrected; and the man who contracts AIDS through homosexuality cannot be cured.

There are, of course, less obvious ways in which the effects of sin continue. There is regret for a wasted life; there is the unhappiness caused by an unequal marriage (Christian and non-Christian); there is the rebellion of children caused by an adulterous relationship. These consequences continue even after there is repentance and restoration of fellowship with God.

These results of sin teach us that sin can never be profitable. In the end it must always bear bitter fruit. The death of Christ shields us from God's wrath (both now and in the hereafter), but it does not erase all of the natural effects of sin experienced in this life. These results also teach us that sin is so serious that it can have effects throughout eternity even for Christians (think of the implications of a poor performance at the judgment seat of Christ).

But now we focus on how God works in the life of an individual believer to point out the destructiveness of sin and the value of remaining in fellowship with the Almighty.

THE ANGUISH OF GUILT

When we grieve the Holy Spirit by sinning, we are immediately aware of it. If not, we have grown hard-hearted in our relationship with God. Guilt that awakens the conscience is usually the first indication that we are out of moral agreement with God. That should lead to confession and the claiming of the cleansing of Christ. "If we confess our sins, he is faithful and just to forgive us our sins and to cleanse us from all unrighteousness" (1 John 1:9, KJV).

However, it is crucial to realize that after we have confessed our sin, guilt has done its work. No longer is guilt used by God as a means to discipline; that would call into question the sufficiency of Christ to forgive and restore us.

Many Christians are in spiritual bondage because they are unable to distinguish the prompting of the Holy Spirit from the accusation of the devil. The Holy Spirit convicts us of sins that we have not brought to God in honest confession. Satan brings accusations to us for those sins even after they have been put away by God. Sins that are "under the blood," as the saying goes, no longer need weigh on our consciences.

Many Christians assume that they must bear the guilt for past sins (though these sins are confessed) as a kind of payment for their misdeeds. They simply do not feel free to enjoy their cleansing, thinking that they do not deserve it.

Of course, we do not deserve it, but that is precisely the meaning of grace! Grace means that we do not get what we deserve. God wipes the slate clean and "remembers our sins no more" (see Hebrews 8:12). For us to remember them, to be controlled by the guilt and power of our memories, is a discredit to the completeness of Christ's work on the cross.

Guilt is God's discipline only until the sin is confessed; any continuation of guilt is the work of Satan. Those accusations must be renounced in the name of Christ.

And what if we do not respond to the immediate prompting of the Holy Spirit? Let us consider those disciplines that are brought into our lives if we persist in deliberate sin. God will put us under pressure designed to bring us to repentance.

THE INTENSIFICATION OF SIN'S POWER

As a pastor I have counseled many men who have been slaves to moral impurity, whether pornography, immorality, or some other addiction. The story is always the same: they began to slide into these sins gradually with halting steps that they believed they could control. But they soon became victimized by the vices they tampered with. God taught them that the sin they took lightly was serious business.

There is a principle seen in both the Old and the New Testament, namely, that we will always be ensnared with the sin we tolerate. God warned Israel that if the nation would serve foreign gods, it would come under the subjection of those foreign powers. "For if you ever go back and cling to the rest of these nations, these which remain among you, and intermarry with them, so that you associate with them and they with you, know with certainty that the Lord your God will not continue to drive these nations out from before you; but they shall be a snare and a trap to you, and a whip on your sides and thorns in your eyes, until you perish from off this good land which the Lord your God has given you" (Joshua 23:12-13).

Read the history of the nation Israel and you will find that they were constantly being subjected to the rule of various nations, even being sold as slaves to them, all because they made alliances with those pagan countries. The compromises we make lead to chains of entrapment and servanthood.

Paul wrote, "Do you not know that when you present yourselves to someone as slaves for obedience, you are slaves of the one whom you obey, either of sin resulting in death, or of obedience resulting in righteousness?" (Romans 6:16). The sin to which we give ourselves is the one that eventually ensnares us. Every time we deliberately sin we degrade ourselves to the role of servants and exalt sin as our master.

Many Christians may confess their sin but are unwilling to make a clean break with the cycle of failure. They are too fearful to seek counsel and keep their secrets to themselves. This incomplete repentance results in further spiritual bondage.

One price of disobedience is slavery.

EMOTIONAL TRAUMA

When Moses warned the people that they would be scattered among the nations if they disobeyed the Lord, he added, "And there shall be no resting place for the sole of your foot; but there the Lord will give you a trembling heart, failing of eyes, and despair of soul" (Deuteronomy 28:65).

This "despair of soul" is further defined: "In the morning you shall say, 'Would that it were evening!' And at evening you shall say, 'Would that it were morning!' because of the dread of your heart which you dread, and for the sight of your eyes which you shall see" (v. 67).

Emotional trauma is often God's way of correction; it is His most persistent discipline of His children. We err if we think that His discipline is always external circumstances. Sometimes, perhaps most often, it is an internal despair that makes even the most significant events of life seem futile.

Is there any New Testament evidence that God uses emotional trauma for His discipline even today?

One of the most difficult and controversial passages in the Bible is Hebrews 10:26-31. The author has just invited believers to draw near to God; he has given them encouragement to stay close to the Savior. Then he writes:

> For if we go on sinning willfully after receiving the knowledge of the truth, there no longer remains a sacrifice for sins, but a certain terrifying expectation of judgment and the fury of fire which will consume the adversaries. Anyone who has set aside the Law of Moses dies without mercy on the testimony of two or three witnesses. How much severer punishment do you think he will deserve who has trampled under foot the Son of God, and has regarded as unclean the blood of the covenant by which he was sanctified, and has insulted the Spirit of grace? For we know Him who said, 'Vengeance is

Mine, I will repay.' And again, 'The Lord will judge His people.' It is a terrifying thing to fall into the hands of the living God.

Many scholars teach that this is a reference to unbelievers, since we read of the harsh judgment that befalls the victims who sin willfully. The consequences appear to be a description of the torments of hell, not the loving rod of a heavenly Father whose children have erred.

Yet there are two reasons that this must be a reference to believers. First, the author includes himself in the possibility of falling into willful sin: "If we go on sinning willfully" (v. 26). Evidently, even he was capable of such a deviation from the Christian path.

Second, the backslider spoken about was sanctified by the blood of the covenant. The text says of him that he is one who "trampled under foot the Son of God, and has regarded as unclean the blood of the covenant by which he was sanctified, and has insulted the Spirit of grace" (v. 29). Clearly, no unbeliever has been sanctified by the blood of the covenant.

The contrast is between the Old Testament, where someone who spurned the mosaic law was put to death, and the New Covenant with its greater privileges and responsibilities. If defiance of an inferior covenant could bring such retribution, what judgment is worthy of the superior covenant? The punishment deserved would obviously be greater.

The people to whom the book of Hebrews was written were tempted to return to the Old Testament sacrifices rather than implicitly trust the blood of the New Covenant. To treat this blood of the covenant as an unholy or common thing was serious indeed. They were turning their backs on the only sacrifice that could save them. Indeed, they could turn to no other effective sacrifice for sins.

This insult to the Spirit of Grace made the breaches of the Old Covenant seem minor in comparison. The penalty in the Old Testament law was frequently death; this kind of rebellion called for a worse punishment.

And what is this worse punishment? The author of the book of Hebrews describes it as "a certain terrifying expectation of judgment, and the fury of a fire which will consume the adversaries" (v. 27). The reference is to God's method of direct judgment frequently used in the Old Testament. The fire should not be thought of as hell, but the temporal fire that took the lives of the disobedient.

God frequently judged His people in the Old Testament by physical death, but that did not mean that all those who were so judged ended in eternal hell. For example, God pardoned the sin of Israel at Kadesh-barnea, and yet that generation was condemned to die in the desert. Physical and temporal judgment can come to those who will experience ultimate salvation.

Thus, in the context in Hebrews we need not read "hell" when we read of "a fury of fire." This judgment, which is as severe as that of the Old Testament (and logically even greater), is the terrifying expectation of judgment and emotional torment that might make physical death seem more tolerable by comparison.

I have counseled believers involved in the sin of adultery who prayed at night that they would not wake up in the morning. Death was more welcome than the emotional trauma they experienced. And, as we shall see later, such discipline may indeed include physical death itself.

Let us not underestimate the severity of God's judgment toward His children. Our understanding of grace must not include the unworthy notion that God is more tolerant today than He was in the Old Testament. He has not grown mellow with age nor changed His mind about a single sin. Under grace the judgment of unbelievers is postponed that they might be brought to repentance (Acts 17:30), but His children experience the effects of His disciplinary hand in this life. "The Lord will judge His people" (Hebrews 10:30). Severity is consistent with grace if its intention is to bring us back into fellowship, that is, to lead us to repentance.

Naturally the question might be asked whether all emotional trauma can be traced to discipline for disobedience. The answer, of course, is no, for the simple reason that emotional distress may have many causes. Some experience it because they were abused as children; others may be going through a time of physical illness or face some tragedy even as Job did. A point that will be emphasized later is that it is not necessary for us to know the precise reason from a trial in order to profit from it.

But there are many believers who can pinpoint their distress to specific acts of disobedience. They can recall when they came to a fork in the road, made a sinful decision, and chose to live with it. The emotional turbulence they have subsequently experienced constantly reminds them that disobedience is not worth the cost. God is speaking, or rather shouting, that they might hear His voice once more.

In keeping with what has been said about the severity of God's judgment, we should not be surprised that God often uses Satan to discipline His children. The evil one is used to inflict the despair of soul, the emotional terror of judgment that is designed to bring God's people back to Him thorough repentance. This is seen both in the Old Testament and the New.

Saul, you will recall, was disobedient to the clear command of God. He was to destroy all of the Amalekites but decided to choose the best of the sheep and oxen and choicest things, along with the king. These he decided to keep for himself and the people. However clever Saul might have appeared to himself, the prophet Samuel was not amused. In fact, the word of the Lord was that God rejected Saul from being king and his kingdom would be given to another.

Saul felt trapped by the decree of God. He deeply resented the fact that his kingdom would be taken from him. He was becoming acquainted with a young man named David who was mightily used of God to slay the giant Goliath. What made matters worse is that the women of Israel honored David when he returned from battle by saying, "Saul has slain his thousands, and David his ten thousands" (1 Samuel 18:7).

Saul deeply resented this unfavorable comparison. He expected David to do what Saul himself would have done in a similar situation, namely, to manipulate to establish himself as king. So we read, "And Saul looked at David with suspicion from that day on" (v. 9).

Jealousy was eating the king alive. Since God had said that the kingdom would be taken away from him, he should have bowed to the will of the Almighty. There was little use fighting the inevitable. But he chose to struggle with God, refusing to acknowledge God's right to give the kingdom to whomever he wished.

God viewed Saul's jealousy as one more act of rebellion. To intensify Saul's irrational moods, the Lord sent an evil spirit to add to his woes. "Now it came about on the next day that an evil spirit from God came mightily upon Saul, and he raved in the midst of the house, while David was playing the harp with his hand, as usual; and a spear was in Saul's hand. And Saul hurled the spear for he thought, 'I will pin David to the wall.' But David escaped from his presence twice" (vv. 10-11).

Saul's paranoia was intensified by an evil spirit from the Lord. Far from being surprised by such a statement, we should realize that all evil spirits are under God's direction. The atmosphere is filled with innumerable evil spirits, who are only too happy to add to the emotional trauma of any human being. Thus for God to permit such a spirit to trouble a person means that the Almighty ordained that it be so.

Why? So that jealousy might become Saul's master. He had, so to speak, made a league with an enemy called envy, and such alliances always lead to spiritual and moral bondage.

This overwhelming presence of evil should have confronted Saul with the enormity of his sin so that he would be brought to utter desperation. That, if Saul were so inclined, would have led him to repentance.

But Saul did not respond favorably to the discipline. His heart became harder, not softer. Instead of throwing himself upon the mercy of God for pardon and deliverance, he chose the path of anger and manipulation. Evidently, he thought that if he were crafty enough he would be able to thwart the revealed plan of God.

Because Saul spurned God's discipline, his life came to a tragic end. He tried to commit suicide but was only partially successful. He had disobeyed God in not exterminating the Amalekites and now, lying wounded, he asked an Amalekite soldier who was running by, to kill him. Thus Saul died at the hand of the enemy he had refused to exterminate! The sin we refuse to put away becomes the sin that eventually destroys us.

To tolerate sin in our lives is like defecting to the enemy in war. This act of treason is welcomed by our adversary the devil and exploited. God supervises, indeed directs, the harassment of Satan as just discipline for persistent sin.

A second illustration comes from the church in Corinth, which was guilty of looking the other way when one of the believers was found to be involved in immoral behavior. Paul admonished the Corinthian believers to excommunicate the offender from the fellowship; indeed Paul himself was prepared to do so though he was not physically present in the fellowship. Here is his exhortation:

> In the name of our Lord Jesus, when you are assembled, and I with you in spirit, with the power of our Lord Jesus, I have decided to deliver such a one to Satan for the destruction of his flesh, that his spirit may be saved in the day of the Lord Jesus. (1 Corinthians 5:4-5)

What does it mean to be "delivered to Satan for the destruction of the flesh"? It meant to be cut off from the spiritual protection of the church. So cut off, this man would be an open target for satanic activity, a pathetic victim of his own sinful choices. That could have eventually led to the destruction of his flesh, that is, physical death. Yet, because he was a believer, his spirit would be saved in the day of Christ.

The man faced a choice as to how he would react. He could harden his heart and continue in immorality, regardless of how seared his conscience became. He could "despise the chastening of the Lord" even to the point of physical destruction.

Or he could do otherwise, namely, seek forgiveness and restoration. He could accept the discipline of the Lord as proper and just, considering the seriousness of the offense. He could choose to put himself under the leadership of the church and follow any procedure they might suggest to heal the wounds his sin had caused. Submission to God's authority would take him out of the realm of Satan's authority.

There is evidence that he chose the latter route. In Paul's second letter, he spoke about an offender's being restored and urged the church to take him back "so that on the contrary you should rather forgive and comfort him, lest somehow such a one be overwhelmed by excessive sorrow. Wherefore I urge you to reaffirm your love for him" (2 Corinthians 2:7-8).

If this is the same man referred to (we cannot be sure), then it is a beautiful example of how God's discipline can lead to restoration.

In my counseling I have met Christians who have dabbled in the occult, only to discover that they received a demonic affliction, the harassment of the devil. Try as they might, they could not easily be freed, even with specific counsel. They were puzzled as to why they were not instantly delivered, since believers have authority over the enemy. I believe the reason was because God was teaching them the "exceeding sinfulness of sin." Easy deliverance, might give the impression that entering Satan's domain is not too serious. God thinks otherwise and uses the struggle for freedom as His means of discipline. Once the freedom comes, the offender is ready to stay clear of such careless (and rebellious) actions.

"That part of us that we rescue from the cross," wrote Tozer, "becomes the seat of our troubles." The sin that we refuse to yield to God is the one that is exploited by Satan so that we might be bound by our own sinful choices. God knows that some backsliders have to be desperate before they cease their rebellion and return to fellowship with Him.

Old Testament examples of people who died because of specific sins are numerous. Nadab and Abihu, the two sons of Aaron, died because they deliberately disobeyed God (Leviticus 10:1-7); Korah and his family opposed God and died (Numbers 16); and Uzzah touched the Ark, and God killed him (2 Samuel 6).

There are New Testament examples, too. Ananias and Sapphira lied to God about their gift to the church, and both died (Acts 5:1-11). Some believers in Corinth died because they partook of the Lord's supper in a flippant way (1 Corinthians 11:30). And the offender in the Corinthian church referred to earlier would have died if he had not repented.

The apostle John wrote that believers should pray for those whose sin does not lead them to death. But then he also adds: "There is a sin leading to death; I do not say that he should make request for this" (1 John 5:16*b*). The "sin unto death" is probably not a specific sin but a certain kind of sin that is so severe it merits the physical death of the individual. We have no idea how many people have died pre-

40

maturely because they did not respond to God's chastening hand.

UNUSUAL BLESSINGS

The idea that God disciplines us through the special gifts of His grace seems inconsistent with all that has been written to this point. But who of us has not been shamed into repentance simply because God blessed us in ways we so clearly did not deserve? One woman said that as a teenager she attended a party where she could have been seduced or even raped. The fact that God protected her from harm (even in the midst of a police raid) led her to such praise to God that she never desired to become involved in such situations again. The hearts of God's people are often won back to Him because of incredible displays of His mercy when they were least expected. Paul taught that the kindness of God is designed to lead unbelievers to repentance; surely this principle applies to believers as well (Romans 2:4).

The bottom line is that God never tolerates sin in the lives of His children. Through the prompting of the Holy Spirit, yes, even through the work of the devil if necessary, He will teach us that sin grieves His heart.

And there are no favorites in His classroom.

41

"My son, do not regard lightly the discipline of the Lord, nor faint when you are reproved by Him" (Hebrews 12:5).

There are three possibilities when we fall under God's disciplinary hand. First, we can take it lightly, that is, disregard it, ignoring the warnings. This, of course, results in great hardness of heart and actually makes further discipline necessary. To regard discipline lightly is to shield ourselves from the lessons God intends to teach us. I have a brother-in-law who was spanked by his father for eating chocolates. Yet even while he was lying across his father's lap receiving his whipping, he reached over and took another one from the box near the couch!

My car has a "Check Engine" light on the control panel. I can ignore it, continue to drive, and get by quite well. But eventually something serious will happen to the motor. If I ignore the warning, I am taking it lightly.

Some people experience great trials and yet never stop to check their spiritual lives to ask, *What is God trying to teach me?* Their sorrows are wasted, or, worse, these people become spiritually insensitive and morally careless.

42

The second possibility is to faint, that is, simply to give up, unable to integrate the trial into a meaningful spiritual experience. Some backslide, deeply bitter with God because of circumstances they believe are unfair. They decide that the fight is not worthwhile.

The third possibility is, of course, to learn from the trial and let it be the means of drawing us closer to God.

How shall we view the trials or disciplines of life? The following points are a guide.

1. *When we experience the trials or disciplines of life, we should ask God to search our hearts to reveal any sins or failures that might be causing the hardship.* This step seems elementary, but is basic to all of our spiritual training. The reason many believers fail to learn from life's disappointments is that they do not give God time to show them what He might be trying to teach them.

The problem of connecting a particular sin with specific discipline is often difficult, sometimes impossible. But we must seek wisdom to know whether God might pinpoint a relationship.

2. *We must not interpret the patience of God as the leniency of God.* If we live with deliberate sin and do not see God's disciplinary hand, we should not deceive ourselves into thinking that

He is ignoring our transgressions. He does not take sin lightly. Many a believer has misjudged the severity of God.

A minister who was involved in adultery said he was totally confused when God continued to bless his ministry despite the ongoing affair. He expected the judgment of God to fall on him for his sin, but it didn't, at least not immediately. People continued to be saved, and the church grew despite this secret liaison.

Of course the disciplinary process had already begun, but he did not realize it. The guilt of the adultery, the lies to cover it, and the fear of exposure were already taking their toll on his personal life. God was not ignoring the sin. He was simply disciplining him on His own schedule. The warning light was blinking furiously, but he ignored it.

Eventually his life and ministry came apart, of course. God's hand upon him was severe. He now knew that his heavenly Father had not overlooked the sin despite His long-suffering. Unfortunately, he had interpreted the long-suffering of God as the indifference of God.

One of the most dangerous experiences we can have is to commit deliberate sin and appear to "get by." That will only develop our confidence to repeat the same sin, expecting the

44

same kind of leniency from the Almighty. There are times when God appears to be indifferent to the sins of His children, but He is only waiting for His correct timing.

The woman who commits adultery without getting pregnant or contracting some form of sexually transmitted disease is being chastened by God just as consistently as the person who commits sin and experiences the other consequences listed above. Not a single one of God's children ever gets by with deliberate sin; chastisement of some kind is absolutely inevitable.

3. *Let us remember that we can learn from every trial whether we know the reason for it or not.* It was not necessary for John and Sally to know whether there was a connection between their deformed baby and premarital sex; William Carey might well have been wrong in making a connection between the fire in his library and his personal failure; the woman who got her divorce on a flimsy pretext may have become ill even if she had remained married. There may have been other ways that God was disciplining them for these failures.

They along with all the rest of us, can learn from every trial, even if we are unsure about a connection between personal sin and our hardships. All trials have a broader purpose:

> Blessed be the God and Father of our Lord Jesus Christ, the Father of mercies and God of all comfort; who comforts us in all our affliction so that we may be able to comfort those who are in any affliction with the comfort with which we ourselves are comforted by God. For just as the sufferings of Christ are ours in abundance, so also our comfort is abundant through Christ. (2 Corinthians 1:3-6)

Every trial is designed to draw us closer to God and to teach us the divine comfort of God. The "trial of our faith is more precious than gold that perishes" (see 1 Peter 1:7, KJV).

Blessed is the person who can accept the hardships of life and grow through adversity.

Blessed is the person who can learn from the burdens of life as well as its blessings.

Moody Press, a ministry of the Moody Bible Institute, is designed for education, evangelization, and edification. If we may assist you in knowing more about Christ and the Christian life, please write us without obligation: Moody Press, c/o MLM, Chicago, Illinois 60610.